MW00625871

Advent, a thread in the night

by E.M. Welcher

Advent, a thread in the night

by E.M. Welcher

To the Fellowship of the Suffering —

Hold on, Beloved.

Resurrection Day Approaches.

Foreword

Ours is a culture that contracts feeling to a small range of superficial and acceptable affections. So we spend much of our life shrunken, shriveled, less alive than we ought to be. The tragedy of that is we spend much of our lives unprepared for Advent. Unready for inbreaking of so much feeling of so many varieties.

Evan Welcher guides us through darkness, through feelings we don't name at dinner parties or even in counseling sessions. He opens us up to ourselves and in doing so opens us up to the glorious good news of Advent. We feel again. We feel a lot. We feel God's presence. Be prepared to *feel* when you read this collection.

Thabiti Anyabwile
Pastor, Anacostia River Church (Washington, DC)

About this book

Horror likes to haunt & hunt me in my heart.

I decided to take the 'lil cuss for a walk in my Twitter neighborhood, every day, for Advent.

December 1st

I n May 2014 my first wife, Danielle, died from Lymphoma, Leukemia, and Venno Occlusive Disease.

As she lay dying I prayed to God through tears, "This is more than I can bear."

And it was. 2014-2017 were desolate, barren, lonesome, cold years of waiting & mourning. Each day I awoke keenly aware of how alone I was in the world.

Anger & self-pity are a heck of a drug. They are rocket fuel for rebellion & all sorts of reckless self-destruction.

I also realized this: that when all else we cherish is stripped away from us, God alone remains. I felt a visceral kinship with Peter's words:

Lord, to whom shall we go? You have words of eternal life. (John 6:68, NASB)

The darkness, the pain, & the cold of Advent is leading somewhere bright and warm, just on the other side of the Magic. If you stretch your hand out far enough during sleepless-phone-holding-nights, you might be able to grasp its warmth. Hold on.

December 2nd

I remember the pain of *Target*.
Walking past the bargain bin she loved so,
And realizing nobody in the world knew where I
was.
No one my soul loved to receive my text:
"I'll be home soon, honey."
How could I be bathed so in such cold, commercial,
fluorescent light...

And still find myself sinking in darkness?

The people who walk in darkness
Will see a great light;
Those who live in a dark land,
The light will shine on them.
(Isa. 9:2, NASB)

Even so, we stretch forth our hands toward
Resurrection.

December 3

During those gloomy years,
I rode my motorcycle too fast
And ate like a teenager.

I'd visit her grave,
And clean her marker with my tears and shirt sleeve.
My bare fingernails fought against encroaching sod.

All of creation groaned with me against this death.

And would nature herself,
Much lauded and idealized,
Encroach upon all our beloved graves
To make the memory of the ignobility of death
faint, and lull us into forgetfulness?

As if we could ever make peace with death here
between the Advents.

There will be no peace here between the worlds to
come until He who cannot forget His beloved
comes with Holy, scarred hands to wipe away tears,

and raise the Dead.

His sheep shall hear His voice.

He still remembers where each is buried.

December 4

We held two funerals for her.
One in Glenwood where she served as the Pastor's wife.

One in St. Louis where she was raised, where she was a history teacher.

History teaches us Jesus had no funeral. For he died a convicted enemy of the state, for our sake.

There were no crowds wailing around Christ's tomb as they had around Lazarus'. All His friends went into hiding.

Except the women. Women driven by compassion and the conviction of the way this world is and is not yet: knew fierce, deep down, that a man deserves a proper burial.

They saw God's wonders.

Yet, Christ had no funeral as she had.

Where people stood up and said all the good she had done, where we were all shocked to discover how many best friends she had.

But every Sunday we gather round a table and testify about all He has done in us.

How when we were Lost He made us Found.

How when were orphans, He adopted us through His Blood and became both our King & Older Brother, who shows us The Way.

How we are but dust, and His mercy knows our frame.

How when we were still His enemies, He Loved us to His own detriment.

She has a lovely monument in an idyllic old graveyard.

I'll know her address on Resurrection Day.

He has no such monument by Resurrection design, but we all carry His ghost around in us like jars of clay, containing an unspeakable weight of glory.

Truly, truly, I say to you, unless a grain of wheat falls into the earth and dies, it remains alone; but if it dies, it bears much fruit. (John 12:24, NASB)

December 5th

One aspect of Danielle's suffering was the loneliness of being immunocompromised. Crowds and germy folk were a real danger. But sometimes, the heart yearns for crowds and germy folks: especially if you love them. The memory of normal: the great was or never was

Haunts.

How she missed shopping, merely walking through a crowd without fear. Church is a crowd. Saints are germy folk, as is the great congregation. Germy & Beloved by God. Germy, and desperately needed.

How The Poet misses God's throng in Psalm 42.

These things I remember, as I pour out my soul: how I would go with the throng and lead them in procession to the house of God with glad shouts and songs of praise, a multitude keeping festival. (Psalm 42:4, NASB)

The Lord Jesus spent forty days and forty nights alone and hungry, and when company came, He was just an accuser & a tempter: a no-good snake...

But when all was said and done,
the Angels came & ministered to the Son of God.

*Then the devil left Him; and behold, angels came and began
to minister to Him.*
(Mat. 4:11, NASB)

Years went by, and Jesus found Himself saying
goodbye to His friends: One Last Supper. They
went out and sang hymns and prayed. Jesus found
Himself surrounded, yet alone, crying out to His
Father, sweating Blood.

*Now an angel from heaven appeared to Him, strengthening
Him.*
(Lk. 22:43, NASB)

The Lord walks with us through the Valley Of The
Shadow Of Death.

We are never alone.

His promise is gravity pulling us Home, until we are
fully & finally never Alone, in the Kingdom of His
Beloved Son.

December 6th

A strangely compassionate doctor noticed how beautiful Danielle's green eyes were. They were filling up with tears as he told us we would never have children. She was wearing her favorite green sweater.

It is strange how dreams are stolen, how we are at times forced to slowly let go of something we Long have yearned for, and Long Loved, just for the dream of Life itself.

She cried hardest of all on that winter day, on my shoulder, in the hospital parking garage, in our run-down Ford Explorer until winter's cold proved too much & she just wanted to go home. I drove through tears and snow, to a home that would never shelter our children.

There was once a young mother.

Her baby was born for all of us, to set us free, and wipe our tears away.

He stomps on death with crucified feet. Wait for the trumpet: He's on His way.

Behold, the virgin shall be with child and shall bear a Son, and they shall call His name Immanuel," which translated means, "God with us."
And Joseph awoke from his sleep and did as the angel of the Lord commanded him, and took Mary as his wife...
(Matthew 1:23–24, NAS)

December 7th

Chemo & Radiation caused sores
In her mouth,
Down her esophagus,
Until she lost so much weight
From the pain of it all,
They put a feeding tube
Through her tummy.

My job was to prepare
A pump full of Osmolite
& keep a journal
Of her caloric intake

This was a culinary duty foreign to me,
A pale shadow of the joy that was once our kitchen.

I sorted pills
By days, by A.M. and P.M.
& filled bags of canned Osmolite.

Jesus is Manna from Heaven,
The true, honest to Himself
For He can swear on nothing higher,

MANNA.

His flesh, true food.
His blood, true drink.
Bread of Heaven,
Everlasting Fount,
Water of Life,
Bubbling Up, Eternal,

The meal, inviting the bedraggled and resigned from
waiting room
to Table.
All washed in His Blood
Shall dine there,
Eat there,
Feast there,
With gaping grins,
Full of food,
Smiling mouths,
Without pain,
Without sores,
Without shame,
On That Day.

December 8th

Danielle spent lifetimes
In waiting rooms,
In hospitals,
In infusion centers,
Attached to IVs,
Walking the halls,
Being pushed down corridors.

Everybody has a story.
Every heart is cracked
And pieced back together,
Daring to beat against the
Gravity of it all.

"In that day," declares the Lord,
"I will assemble the lame
And gather the outcasts,
Even those whom I have afflicted.
I will make the lame a remnant
And the outcasts a strong nation,
And the Lord will reign over them in Mount Zion
From now on and forever." (Micah 4:6–7, NASB)

December 9th

She had a 10,000 Mega Watt smile
With which
She disarmed & blessed the world
And made all things well,

If you could make her smile.

Chemo discolored her pride & Joy.
Mouth sores made brushing her teeth a test of
endurance,

Yet, I saw her, every day, brace herself

Against the sink with her free arm
And slowly, brush her teeth,
Deliberately, with bald head bowed
In prayer & pain,
Methodically brushing her teeth, a rebellion against
the darkness,
A liturgy of resistance,
That the faithful
Would bring forth the advent

Of Life

As we once knew it,
As we once took for granted.
All these normal things we never thought deeply about
Would be the reward of surviving.

Perhaps Jesus' gift to us all was that His ordinary Life of faithful obedience turned out to be the most extraordinary Life of them all.

Perhaps the greatest assault you can launch against the darkness is to put your two weary feet on the cold morning floor
& Rise.[1]

Faithful is He who calls you, and He also will bring it to pass. (1 Thes, 5:24, NASB)

---

[1] As John Blasé says in his poem, *The Bravest Thing*

December 10th

When someone you love is taken away from you, the world keeps on spinning wildly through the indifferent cosmos. Time marches on. You don't.

Or you do.

But you never stop wondering what they would think about this or that, after all: we shared a life.

Who would she be today, who *is* she today? What would she have thought had she lived? What does she think now?

Danielle died in 2014. She taught middle school history near Ferguson, Missouri. What would she have thought about all the pain and division we have all grown used to today?

She was a missionary teacher in her beloved South Sudan. What would she think about the continuing strife born out of such promise?

Somehow Advent is the indwelling of Hope from carnage, the blooming of possibility from scorched earth.

A phoenix rising from ashes.

And Simeon blessed them and said to Mary His mother, "Behold, this Child is appointed for the fall and rise of many in Israel, and for a sign to be opposed—and a sword will pierce even your own soul—to the end that thoughts from many hearts may be revealed." (Lk. 2:34-35, NASB)

December 11th

 remember one time
Danielle's Oncologist
Kept us waiting in the examination Room so long,
we thought we'd lose our minds and crawl up the
walls.
We thought about Ghosting,
Wondered if she had Ghosted us,

So I did silly impressions until she laughed so hard
that her biopsy incisions ached.

And she sang flip songs until I laughed so hard my
heart ached over from how much I loved her &
how little I could do to help her.

Over how much I wanted to save and spare her, but
couldn't.

I'm not sure what Love is other than Jesus Christ,
Crucified For People Who Hate Him.

Maybe it's your heart beating outside your body in
another's chest.

But there's a baseball sized tumor pressing hard.

Maybe it's holding her hand, wiping her tears and just staying,

Come Hell or high water,
Because there are no bad guys to kill,
Just cruel fate to endure.

I adore Jesus, my King, my Savior, my Lord, my Friend...

I envy Him.

For when He wanted to save the people He Loved, He was able to do something. He was able to trade Himself,

But I was

Forced to watch
Cruel Death
Take & Take & Take.

The coldest fire burning forever in my gut 'til Resurrection Day
Will always be that I couldn't save her.

It only hurts when I think about it.

But on that day we laughed until it hurt.

We Loved until it hurt.

And the Doc finally arrived, apologizing: relieved to find us in such merry spirits.

The Light shines in the darkness, and the darkness did not comprehend it.
(Jn. 1:5, NASB)

December 12th

T he Lord Jesus said, in the last times, the Love of many will grow cold. (Mt. 24:12)

And my, don't we see it?
Don't it pull us down,
Deflate us,
A weight on our chests,
Breaking our hearts?

Here in this sorrow,
Here in this shadow

We need Testimony.

I saw my Resplendent Bride
Endure.
I saw Her *plunged to victory*
Beneath the cleansing flood.[2]

She endured bone marrow biopsies.
She endured Chemo.

---

[2]From E.M. Bartlett's hymn: *Victory in Jesus*

She endured Radiation.
She endured a port and feeding tube.
She endured nausea & mouth sores.
She endured neuropathy & infertility.

Danielle endured.
Danielle kept the faith.

And she never cursed God.

Or His Church for that matter.

Danielle blooms in Resurrection Forever.

And Mary said:
"My soul exalts the Lord,
And my spirit has rejoiced in God my Savior.
"For He has had regard for the humble state of His
bondslave;
For behold, from this time on all generations will count me
blessed.
For the Mighty One has done great things for me;
And holy is His name.
And His mercy is upon generation after generation
Toward those who fear Him."
(Lk. 1:46–50, NASB)

December 13th

nd Still
The Light Shines.

December 14th

Walking with her through the desolation of
cancer felt like
Years of winter.

And when she closed her eyes
For the last time,
Desolation set in.

We had fought side by side
For years.

Now my brother
Drove me home
Across the prairie,
Bleak & barren.

What had it all been for?

Every death,
Loved one or stranger,
Every last death

Is an eschatological event.

Every last breath
An ellipsis...

Resurrection Shall Bloom.
On Every Grave,
Resurrection Shall Bloom.

But when these things begin to take place, straighten up and lift up your heads, because your redemption is drawing near. (Lk. 21:28, NASB)

December 15th

We held her funeral at the Little White Church I Pastored.
All these years later, I'm still there.

I only half joke that I want to be buried under the Communion Table.

Last week, Delores stood up with tears at the Women's Christian Society Lunch

And reminded everybody that I am the longest serving Pastor in the 162 year history of the Church.
Delores is the Church historian, after all.

This little White Church Loves Advent. Sure, they like singing Christmas songs during Advent, and they forget to change the paraments,

And even light the candles out of order,

But they love the mystery,
Holding it with a good conscience even.
And they have seen their fair share of death.
And they wait for Resurrection Day

With bated breath.

And she who is forgiven much
Loves much.

Selah.

December 16

And still the light shines.
Hold on, Beloved.
Hold on.

December 17th

Before Danielle's final hospitalization, she complained to the White Coats of her distended abdomen.

"Constipation" from pain killers they said.

But she insisted something else was going on.

She was right. It was Venno Occlusive Disease. Her liver was damaged from the very chemo meant to save her life and make the bone marrow transplant possible. Her abdomen was filling with her own unclean blood, causing a cascade of organ failure and the fading of her mind.

I cannot help regretting everything, and reproaching myself, and asking, "What if?" things had been done differently. What if she had been believed? What if I had held the White Coat's feet to the fire?

What if they had kicked the psychologist off her medical team and just given her the bone marrow transplant earlier?

Reproach & regret have been my constant
companions all this time.

Can you ever forgive me?

Deliver me from the mire and do not let me sink;
May I be delivered from my foes and from the deep waters.
May the flood of water not overflow me
Nor the deep swallow me up,
Nor the pit shut its mouth on me.
Answer me, O Lord, for Your lovingkindness is good;
According to the greatness of Your compassion, turn to me,
And do not hide Your face from Your servant,
For I am in distress; answer me quickly.
Oh draw near to my soul and redeem it;
Ransom me because of my enemies!
You know my reproach and my shame and my dishonor;
All my adversaries are before You.
Reproach has broken my heart and I am so sick.
And I looked for sympathy, but there was none,
And for comforters, but I found none.
(Psalm 69:14–20, NAS)

If you weep amongst the graves, deep into the late
watches of the night, the only light you may see are
the stars of heaven twinkling with eternal innocence,
hinting that a brighter day is waiting with bated
breath to dawn. And should there be cloud cover,
you will need faith.

Long ago, a star guided desperate, searching men to a house, and in it was a toddler, innocent enough to bear all our reproach & shame, on a day when darkness fell upon all the land, and the earth quaked and the dead rose from their graves.

He brings the Light
With Him.

December 18th

After the flame of her candle was snuffed
out in the spring of life,

I spent night after night sleeping on the old couch
that sat in the converted porch we called our living
room, surrounded by wilting condolence flowers
and stacks of sympathy cards.

There was no heat in that room.
There in the lingering shadow of death, I figured
Morning neck aches and midnight shivers were
The price we pay to stay
Here in the land of the living.

And the sun always rose
Day after day,
A ball of flame,
Burning in the east.

Not long after she went Home
To be with the Lord forever,
A young couple wanted a widower to bless their
union with broken hearted words on Love, so I did.

Then I hopped on my Bicycle and rode it across the
Everlasting rolling Hills of Iowa.

In the July heat I could weep in the midday Sun
and the mob was none the wiser.
Tears & Sweat are all the same,
And nobody knew my name
Or story,
Or asked how I was doing
Or how
I felt.

Just keep pedaling
To the next town.
Eat and sleep,
And whatever you do,
Never. Stop. Pedaling.

No hill lasts forever.

But He does.
Jesus lasts Forever.
And somewhere under His everlasting arms,
Under the shelter of His wings,
I built my Ebenezer
And tilled my garden.
Winter
planting.
Growing
harvest.

Year after year,
Singing in the House Of The Lord.

Resurrection Follows Him.

December 19th

nd still
The Light
Shines,

A Star
Guiding
Us Home
To Resurrection.

December 20th

When you are dying
In the cancer ward,
They move you into the big room
So people can visit you
In your coma.

She died surrounded by her family.
There was Love.
There was Horror.

She was Resplendent all her days
And death is an unnatural enemy,
An alien force,

Preying upon the planet
The Lord declared "Good,"
Long before the breaking of the world.

I have my memories
They warm & chill,
Keep me going, slay me.

I prayed endlessly for her healing.

Some said:
"Pray More.
Pray Better.
Pray Right.
Have this person Pray.

Oh, if only you had MORE..."

Sometimes
Some kind
Of believers
Will cut you deepest.

They're still at it too,
From the T.V. to the Red Woods Of California.

They make Enemies of Brethren
By holding our beloved, faithful
Dead Against Us.

We're all desperate for Life,
And they prey on prayer.

But none of this is about them.
This is about Jesus

He who died
&
Rose three days later.

This is Advent,
The waiting & mourning time.
Our whole being,
Up until Resurrection Day,
Occurs in the waiting room
Of His three days in Jonah's Big Fish.
Our entire lives in three thin, bereft days.
Death Looms Large.
Death Is Already Defeated.
All that remains
Are the Fireworks.

Beloved, I fervently prayed for healing, but not
Resurrection Before Christ's say so.

Sometimes the boldness of faith
Means waiting with bated breath,
Clinging to the word Resurrection
With your nails & teeth,
For it is all we ever had.
The Boldness Of Faith
Is obedience Now,

In the here & now, while we wait
And wait, O, Beloved, faithfulness is waiting with
tear stained cheeks
And not a word left in your mouth,
Righteous arms lifted
Awaiting the coming of the King,
And all the ones Death stole,
Coming Home to creation good

And restored
In His wake.

But we do not want you to be uninformed, brethren, about those who are asleep, so that you will not grieve as do the rest who have no hope.
For if we believe that Jesus died and rose again, even so God will bring with Him those who have fallen asleep In Jesus.
For this we say to you by the word of the Lord, that we who are alive and remain until the coming of the Lord, will not precede those who have fallen asleep.
For the Lord Himself will descend from heaven with a shout, with the voice of the archangel and with the trumpet of God, and the dead in Christ will rise first.

(1 Thes. 4:13-16, NASB)

December 21st

 nd here things begin to brighten.
The tide begins to turn.
The planet turns just so,
Just right,

And Immanuel's people
Have lit just enough
Candles

That we see the light
Bursting forth,
There! Yonder
Over the hills,
Bordering
The Everlasting Prairie.

Imagine Israel,
Long enslaved,
Walking through the darkness
Of the Red Sea,
Torn asunder by Wonder,
Stepping toward
mystery swirling ahead,

Better than the darkness we leave behind,
Better than Chariots & Lash,
And endless unyielding quota.

I'll take the raging wild of Yahweh's unknown
Sovereignty
Over the oppressive darkness I leave behind.
Lead us Home.
Cloud by day,
Pillar of fire
By Night.

Jesus is Advent Manna Enough
For your people,
Sojourning here,
Journeying to Beulah Land.
Weary, we
Wash up at your Table.

Sweet Lord,
You took on flesh to die,

A super nova
In eschatological darkness.

The Star Dust of your Incarnation
Leaves crumbs,
leading us Home
Through the dark forest of suffering.

Make me to hear joy and gladness,
Let the bones which You have broken rejoice.
Hide Your face from my sins
And blot out all my iniquities.
Create in me a clean heart, O God,
And renew a steadfast spirit within me.
Do not cast me away from Your presence
And do not take Your Holy Spirit from me.
Restore to me the joy of Your salvation
And sustain me with a willing spirit.

(Ps. 51:8–12, NASB)

December 22nd

 saiah 7

The King in Jerusalem,
Shaking like a tree in the wind
Beset on all sides by enemies.

God says, ask a sign,
Any sign.
Low as the land of the dead,
High as Heaven.
Before this child is old enough
To know how bad things are,

I'll show you just how much
God Is With You.

When Matthew wanted to write down all that he
had seen and heard
With his friend Jesus:

How at the beginning
Of Incarnation
When

good old St. Joe
Had very real fears of betrayal,
The Angel said have no fear.

This boy will save His people.
He really is God With Us.

God With Us.
In the lonely & the thin,
In the lawyer's office,
In the hospital waiting room,
Bedside & graveside,
God With Us.
When you are fearsome enough,
To go to Church Alone,

When everything,
breaks wide open,
Behind & ahead,

God Is With You.

December 23rd

Long lay our hearts
In everlasting gloom.
Darkness and barren earth
Loom
Large beneath Scorched sky,

And still...

From it we await a Savior.

Come, O Come,
Immanuel,

Daystar,

Avenger of Martyrs,

Establisher Of The Kingdom.

O Come,

LORD Of All That IS.

We yearn,

We wait,
Working quietly with these
Rough hands.

Will grace yet smooth our abrupt edges,
Without cutting a single corner?
Carpenter King:
Build us out of the stuff

That lasts.
Resurrection,
Resurrection
At Long Last.
Make all things right.
Slaughter Death
Before Our Eyes.
Make The Kingdom
Theocratic.
Make Heaven & Earth New.

Eden Restored. Better.

For You Are The Old Magic.

Maranatha.

And all whom
We have long mourned,
Whose memory we nurtured
With long walks in shadowy wood,
Snapshots of the past,

Fading yet painstakingly colored
In the museum of our hearts,

May they burst forth from the grave
On that day!
May heaven be darkened
With a rain shower
Of tombstone.

*For just as the lightning comes from the east and flashes even
to the west, so will the coming of the Son of Man be.
"Wherever the corpse is, there the vultures will gather."*
(Mt. 24:27–28, NASB)

December 24th

 Come Let Us Adore Him,
Lord At His Birth.

Let the weary and bedraggled
Come in from the wastelands
And say:

Won't He Do It?
Is He Not Faithful?

We Still Believe.
Yes, Even Now
The King Is Arriving.
Will He Not Finish All Of This?

He Is Still With Us.

Lord Jesus,
Crucified Carpenter King,
You're Home.

Acknowledgements

Thank you, Michaela O'Neal, for bringing the darkness to life on paper.

Thank you to my Rachel Pie
for Loving Me in the Darkness,
and editing my ruins.

Interior artwork

Michaela J. O'Neal is a Jill of many trades and master of none, a dabbler in photography, words, art, music, plants, and anything that has beauty. She can be found on Instagram or Twitter @reformingjoy but also in the hills of Northern California where she is learning how to look to Jesus in everything, and how to live each day in the piercing light of eternity.

Cover art and book editor

Rachel Joy Welcher (MLit, University of St. Andrews) is a columnist and editor at *Fathom* magazine. She is the author of two books of poetry: *Blue Tarp* and *Two Funerals, Then Easter*, and also writes about theology, most recently addressing sexual ethics in her book: *Talking Back to Purity Culture: Rediscovering Faithful Christian Sexuality* from *InterVarsity Press*. She lives in Glenwood, Iowa, with her husband, Evan.

Evan Welcher is the senior pastor of Vine Street Bible Church in Glenwood, Iowa. After losing his wife to cancer, Evan wrote the book *Resplendent Bride*, chronicling the love and loss of his first marriage, and has recently published a collection of poems called *Nightscapes: poetry from the depths*. He lives with his wife, Rachel, and their dog, Frank, in a house on a hill.

Made in the USA
Monee, IL
19 November 2020